THE ANGL

"The best waterside ..."

A Waveney Valley Path from Norfolk Broads to Suffolk Brecks.

Linking Weavers' Way, Wherryman's Way, Peddars Way, Icknield Way and Iceni Way.

Including accommodation and public transport information.

Published by The Ramblers' Association
Registered Charity 1093577

Norfolk & Suffolk Areas

First edition - September, 1989
Second edition - February, 1990
Third edition - January, 1991
Fourth edition - February, 1993
Fifth edition - September, 1995
Sixth edition - February, 2000
Seventh edition - June, 2001
Eighth edition - December, 2005

CONTENTS

Page 3	Introduction - First Edition
Page 4	Introduction - Current Edition
Page 5	The Route
Page 20	Mileage Chart and Transport Planner
Page 22	Accommodation and Amenities List
Page 28	Connecting Long Distance Paths

The maps are reproduced from Ordnance Survey based mapping on behalf of The Controller of Her Majesty's Stationery Office, © Crown copyright 100033886 2005

Additional information, such as hedges and fences, based on a survey carried out by the Ramblers' Association has been included in our maps.

There should be sufficient detail in this guide for you to follow the waymarked path, but wider knowledge of the area can be obtained from O.S. Maps 1:25,000 scale - Explorer Nos. OL40, 231 and 230.

The route is a pleasant one and could be used for short circular walks with the aid of the O.S. Maps. Another useful idea is to co-operate with friends, using two cars, parking one at your chosen finishing point and taking the other to where you would like to start.

Public transport is frequent between Great Yarmouth and Bungay, but elsewhere it is sparse or non existent. Some hotels, guest houses, etc. are willing, by prior arrangement, to pick you up from the route and return you to the same spot the next morning - see the accommodation list for details.

On completion of the Way at Knettishall Heath you may make arrangements with friends or a taxi, walk to Thetford (via A1066) or Harling Road railway stations or consider the limited additional options shown on pages 20 and 21. Alternatively you may extend the route, using the first 16 miles of the Iceni Way, not the shortest route to Thetford, but certainly the most enjoyable.

Any comments you may have on this booklet will be welcome and should be sent to: Sheila Smith, Caldcleugh, Cake Street, Old Buckenham, Attleborough, Norfolk, NR17 1RU.

THE ANGLES WAY

Introduction to First Edition

The search for the source of the world's great rivers has always been an enticing project. But without pretence to such alluring heights, the desire to follow the Waveney Valley to its source by footpaths, bridleways and byways was the original motivation for this route. Subsequently the horizons were broadened, and the route extended to form an attractive link between Peddars Way and Knettishall Heath and Weavers Way at Great Yarmouth.

The Waveney forms the border between Norfolk and Suffolk, so it was ideal that both Areas of the Ramblers' Association should join in the promotion of the route, and to this purpose a working committee, with representatives from each Area, was formed in 1986 to discuss, survey and finalise the subsequent route for publication.

It was perhaps fortuitous that an "Upper Waveney Valley" project to open up the area for leisure and recreation was formulated by Mid-Suffolk District Council at about this time, and eventually joined and supported by Norfolk and Suffolk County Councils and all the adjoining District Councils, together with the Countryside Commission and other interested organisations. Liaison with this representative body brought recognition and support for the proposed Path, and the continued involvement of all interested parties has ironed out most of the initial problems, together with many that have subsequently arisen, resulting in a much enhanced route. The continued examination of possible improvements and their implementation will provide an even better Way in the future, truly worthy of the Waveney and the upper reaches of the Little Ouse.

As producers of this route guide we take no credit for creation, since both the Valley and the paths were already in existence long before their amalgamation into what we called the Waveney Valley Path, now designated The Angles Way, but we hope that you will experience the ever changing countryside of the broadland, marsh, riverside and East Anglian farmland. Under the wide skies of the region there is much to offer the walker, whatever the interest, not least its historical associations, from Roman ruins at Burgh Castle, medieval castles at Bungay, Mettingham and Wingfield, numerous manor houses and the much debated origins of the Minster of South Elmham for, as one contemporary writer has stated the Waveney Valley is a "real cradle of history".

Enjoy your walking and remember the Country Code.

B.J. SWATMAN - Chairman - Waveney Valley Path Committee
Norfolk & Suffolk Areas - Ramblers' Association
September, 1989

Introduction to Current Edition

Since the Angles Way was first devised there have been several alterations and improvements to the route. Opportunities, such as provision of new bridges, have enabled us to include rights of way which were previously unusable as through routes. Thus we no longer have a mile along the A1066 at Bressingham, this improvement, involving a substantial alteration to the route resulted from the installation of new bridge over the Waveney and the creation of a short right of way in Suffolk to connect with an existing one in Norfolk.

The bypasses on the A140 and A143 to avoid first Scole and then Brockdish required amendments to our route, partly to conform with essential changes in the rights of way system and partly to ensure that we keep as far away as possible, for as long as possible from those busy new sections of road.

When the Angles Way was opened it was 77 miles long, the amendments have added a bit and subtracted a bit, but the net result is just one extra mile.

No doubt there will be further alterations in the future, some will be thrust upon us, others will be sought, planned and negotiated for by the Ramblers, or by Norfolk and Suffolk County Councils and other local authorities involved. During the sixteen years since the Angles Way was first opened local government officers and Ramblers' Association volunteers, not always agreeing, but respecting each others' views, have worked together so that the route continues to evolve and improve.

In 2003 our route was selected by Waterscape (a part of British Waterways) as the "Best waterside walk in Britain", we always knew how special it is, but is good to have this view endorsed!

SHEILA SMITH Editor - Angles Way Committee

December, 2005   Norfolk & Suffolk Areas - Ramblers' Association

ACKNOWLEDGEMENTS: Without the work of the Angles Way Committee (formerly the Waveney Valley Path Committee), formed by Norfolk and Suffolk members of the Ramblers' Association, this description and accommodation list would never have appeared in print.

The original Committee comprised: Basil Swatman, Chairman; Sheila Smith, Secretary; George le Surf, Editor; Charles Barker, Treasurer; Pat Rattenbury, Cartographer; Jill Thompson, Alan Bowell and Stephen Hewitt who surveyed and advised.

The present Committee comprises: John Sayer, Chairman; Peter Westmacott, Secretary; Sheila Smith, Treasurer and Editor; Alan Bowell, Derek Goddard, Brenda Le Grys and George le Surf.

Contributions were also made by Roger Wolfe, who designed the mileage and transport chart. Jeanne le Surf (now Norfolk Area President, formerly County Footpath Secretary), provided valued and expert advice. D. Urquhart of Lowestoft drew the front cover illustration.

Our thanks are due to them all.

Great Yarmouth is a popular resort with long stretches of sandy beach and popular amusements along its sea front including summer shows on its piers. Good shopping streets and a well-stocked market place will supply most needs. There is a maritime museum of great interest and the house of Anna Sewell authoress of Black Beauty.

The route starts at Vauxhall Station where a sign post marks the junction of the Weavers' Way, Wherryman's Way and Angles Way, notice boards give outlines of the routes. *(The Weavers' Way has been extended to the sea front near the pier.)*

NOTE: Pedestrian access is permitted over Breydon lift bridge but it is not encouraged. Well worn tracks exist up the embankments.

Leave the station, cross the River Bure by footbridge (formerly a rail-way bridge to the docks), turn right and follow the road to Haven Bridge. Cross the Haven Bridge *(you will see the second longest quay in Europe after Rotterdam.)* At the junction of Steam Mill Lane is an Angles Way notice board. Go along Steam Mill Lane to a left bend then along short fenced path ahead into Crittens Road. Go ahead past a play area to the end of the road and to a new footpath passing the entrance of a boatyard. Continue past the boatyard, then bear right onto another new path leading up to the flood defence wall. Follow path wall under Breydon Lift Bridge and along the edge of Breydon Water to a jetty and a double gate.

Breydon Water is controlled by the RSPB, with some preserved wildfowlers' rights. In winter it provides feeding and roosting areas for waders and wild-fowl: Bewick's and mute swans, Brent geese, wigeon, pintail, teal, lapwing, golden plover, curlew and dunlin. In spring come migrants: greenshank, black tailed godwit, avocet, spoonbill and black tern. Shelduck and common tern breed in abundance. Predators include kestrel, marsh and hen harriers, their tense grace contrasting with awkwardly flapping heron and cormorant. Visitors include Sandwich tern and great grey shrike. In summer waders like sandpiper and Temminks stint feed upon invertebrates in the shallows.

After half a mile go through a double gate and continue on the bank for about two miles, through more double gates, until the bank turns sharply right. Continue on the bank to the next gate. Berney Mill will be in view, ahead on the far side of the river.

NOTE Breydon Wall disabled access route runs from the car park by the jetty. The double gates permit wheelchair access and prevent cattle getting through.

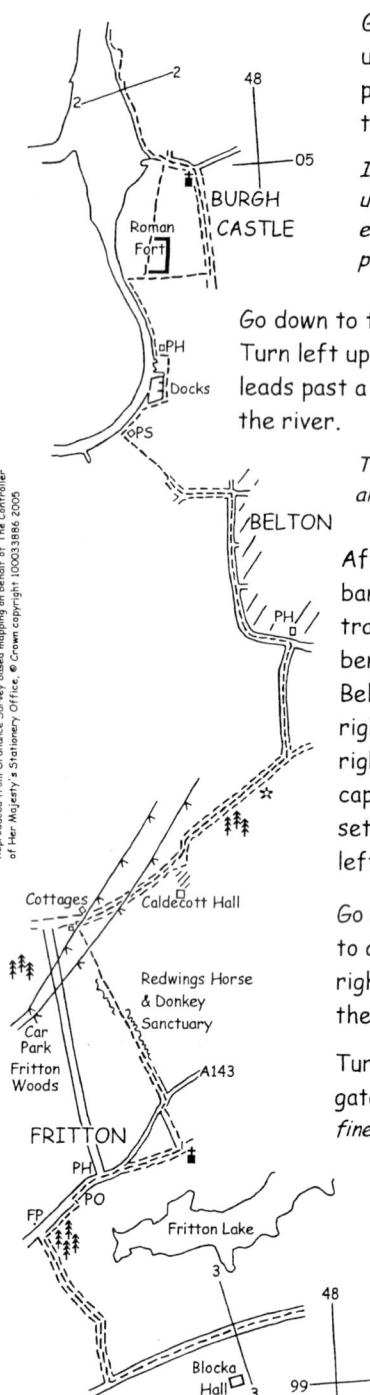

Go through the gate and the bank leads into a path uphill to Burgh church (or turn right and follow a path along the marsh). Take the lane on the left of the church to the Roman fort.

In the Roman fort of Burgh rested the Dalmatian cavalry under the Count of the Saxon Shore. The Broads did not exist in those days, only a great bay called Gariensis protected by Burgh and its opposite fort in Caister.

Go down to the riverbank and turn left to the Fisherman's Rest. Turn left uphill a short way, then turn right in a footpath which leads past a harbour, with a fence on your right and returns to the river.

The rivers of East Anglia are full and slow, bringing trade and prosperity deeply inland.

After a short way, by a small pumping station on the bank, turn left down to a stile and over into a green track to another stile. Cross into a lane which soon bends left for a rough walk to a road on a corner in Belton. Turn right for $3/4$ mile to the Tavern and turn right into Sandy Lane. After a while the lane bends right and becomes truly sandy as you pass a pine capped hill on your left. After you pass under the 2nd set of national grid lines and just past a cottage, turn left into a path on the left of the next cottage.

Go straight over a field to a hedge, follow a right edge to a gap. Turn left and immediately right to follow a right edge until a gap brings you back to the left of the hedge, then into a track and out to a road.

Turn right for 80 yards, then left through a kissing gate and straight to Fritton Church. *It is one of the finest surviving Saxon churches in England.*

Turn right in a sunken lane to the A143, go left, then just beyond a PO take a permissive path on the left, following the road behind the hedge. Near a hilltop, turn left again into a track with trees on its left and near a pole with a transformer. The track leads to another road, turn left and, just beyond Herringfleet Hall, turn right through a gateway into a field.

Follow a right edge, but as it bends sharply right you turn left to the field edge where you turn right and along a left edge to a road. Turn right a short way, then left in a track to Ashby Church. Turn right in a track past the church to a crossing hedged track and turn right to a road. Turn left to road junction by Somerleyton Park. Take the road for Blundeston to another junction, go ahead for the station, but when the road bends right, for Duke's Head, turn left by a phone box. Take the right fork to the end of a line of garages.

Go leftwards into a boatyard (the route may be obscured by boats). Follow waymarks past dyke head, keeping to the left of offices, go through a gap in the hedge in the corner of the boatyard.

Turn left on a track, then right on a path to another track. Go right and follow the track past cottages to a road leading to Somerleyton station. Turn left, up the hill to a 'T' junction at Waveney Grange Farm and right into a hedged lane.

When the lane forks take the lower path, meeting another lane in less than a $1/2$ mile. Turn right, in about 200 yards turn right again, taking a footpath through a wooded area. *(Some OS maps show the alternative route).* Over a stile into another lane, cross, follow field edge path, continue in this direction, with hedge on the right, to reach another lane. Turn right passing high gabled cottages.

Turn left along a marsh edge with a ditch on left for a $1/4$ mile to a footbridge, cross and follow a bank through woodland carr to another bridge.

Cross, and turn right in a field, follow the path to a marsh road. Turn left, but soon, as the road bends sharply left, turn right and through an iron gate into a marsh. Turn left along the edge to a stile and over into a green track. Turn left to meet a road in Camp's Heath. Turn right to a telephone box and fork right, past a farm, into a track which meets another below Oulton Church.

Continue your direction to a fork and turn left, uphill, to the church. Take the path on the right for Prospect Road and follow to its end.

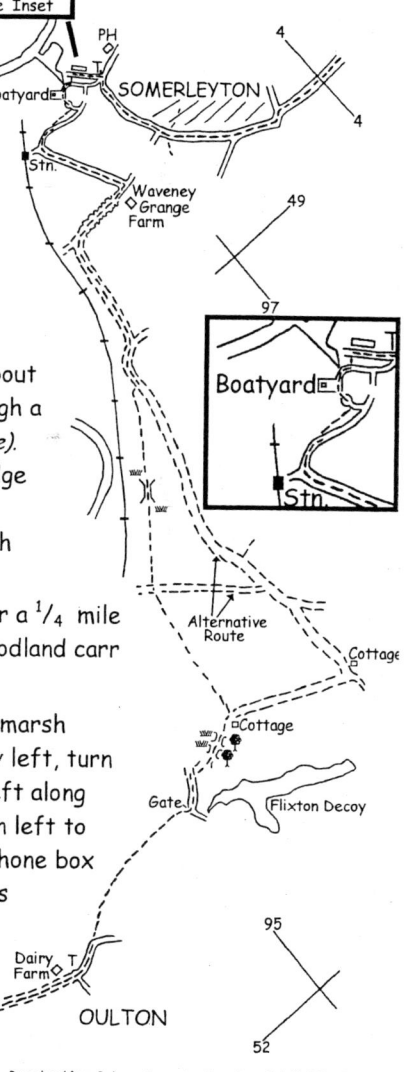

Reproduced from Ordnance Survey based mapping on behalf of The Controller of Her Majesty's Stationery Office, © Crown copyright 100033886 2005

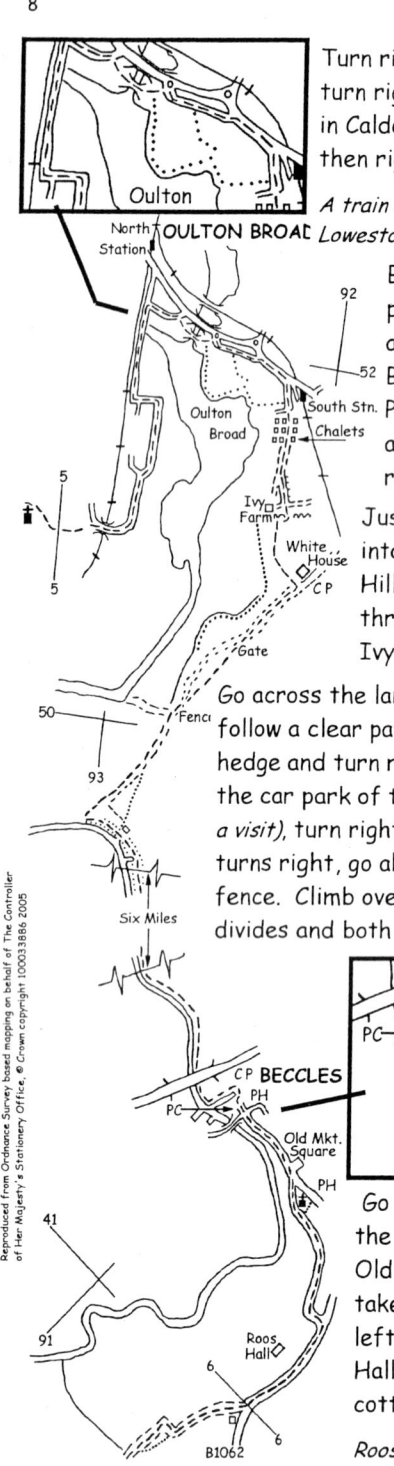

Turn right, go over a railway bridge, follow Borrow Road, turn right along Romany Road to The Maltings, turn left in Caldecote Road to follow the railway and turn right, then right again into Commodore Road to its end.

A train service is available from Oulton Broad North into Lowestoft for an overnight stay.

Bear right across hotel car park entrance, follow path with dual cycle track, continue over footbridge across Mutford Lock. Follow the road past Oulton Broad boat quay and entrance of Nicholas Everitt Park, for about ¾ mile. When the park is open other attractive routes are available rejoining the main route near the chalets.*

Just before Oulton Broad South station turn right into Marsh Road, keeping right to a F.P. sign for Burnt Hill Lane on a sharp right bend. Follow a clear path through a chalet site*, westwards to meet a lane near Ivy Farm.

Go across the lane and over a wooden fence into a meadow and follow a clear path across it. Go through a gap in a crossing hedge and turn right into a path round a field edge. Go through the car park of the Suffolk Broads and Wildlife Centre (*well worth a visit*), turn right and follow Burnt Hill Lane, but, when the track turns right, go ahead through a gate towards a double wooden fence. Climb over and straight ahead to the river bank (the path divides and both lead to the bank).

Turn left for seven miles into Beccles. When you reach the Quay turn right over a wooden footbridge and right again.

Go left at the Broads Information Centre towards the town into Northgate and turn right opposite the Old Market Square (or continue past the church and take a path on its left) down into Puddingmoor. Turn left and join the B1062. Turn right, passing Roos Hall, take a sandy track on your right by a pair of cottages.

Roos Hall is a fine example of Tudor architecture.

Follow the winding track to a bridge. Cross and continue, as Barsham Church tower appears on your left, to a sandy track by cottages.

Catherine Suckling, mother of Lord Nelson, was born in the Jacobean rectory. The church has an unusual lattice design enclosing the windows in the east wall.

Cross into a grassy track and along field edges, at the end of the second field cross a stile and go ahead for a few yards then right over another stile. Follow the right edge, then as the fence curves to the left go over a stile onto a wooded path, then continue along an open track.

A detour across the marsh and over a footbridge connects with Locks Lane and leads to Geldeston. The Locks Inn is close to the river. Go over a stile, pass a large pumping station and continue along an access road, bending to the left, then turn right onto a green lane just beyond a cottage.

The lane passes through a gateway, with a stile alongside and, about 25 yards before you reach two gates ahead, and almost opposite another gate on your right, turn left over a plank bridge and a stile into a field. Turn right and cut the right corner to another stile, do not cross, but turn up the right edge of the field to another stile in a corner.

Cross and continue along the right edge of a garden to the Beccles/Bungay road in Shipmeadow.

Turn right, continue past a drive on your left leading to converted workhouse buildings, now called Viewpoint, and take the next headland.

Keeping the hedge on your right follow the edge which bends and turns eventually down to a corner of the field. Turn right and follow left edges, eventually bending left to a lane opposite a farm.

Turn right to a road junction on a corner. Continue your direction and, about 100 yards past a pair of cottages on your right, turn right into a green hedged lane. (*This is a permissive path which is closed at Christmas*).

Walkers will shortly join the Bigod Way, which takes its name from the family which built and owned the castle in Bungay.
Follow the lane to its end and over into another lane to a road on a corner. Go ahead and when the road bends right continue your direction into a bridleway and down to the Beccles/Bungay road at Watch House Hill. Turn left to the bottom of the hill and turn right for Ditchingham.

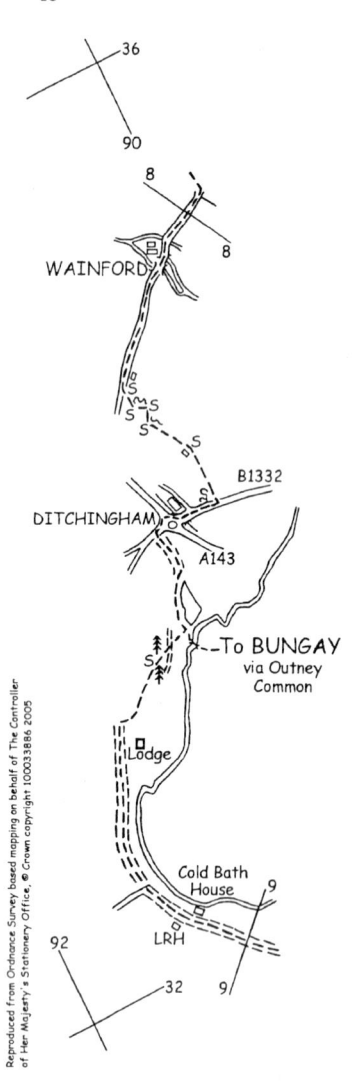

The road soon leads across the Waveney and past a mill for about $1/2$ mile, then turn left over a stile immediately past some houses. Cut a right corner of a field to the next stile. Cross and turn along a left edge to another stile in a corner.

Cross and turn right to a stile and over into the next field. Turn left and, moving away from the left edge, go to a stile on the left of huts. Cross and along a right edge to the next stile. Go over and leftwards to a gate and out to a road. Turn right and at a road junction, go ahead past a ruined mill and over a humped bridge to a roundabout. Take the B1332 and immediately turn left in a stony track to a large flooded pit.

Bear rightwards in a path along a field edge and into trees and, shortly after it bends left, you turn right *(do not turn here if you wish to visit Bungay, but carry straight on over the Waveney and straight across Outney Common)*. Go a short way to a wooden kissing gate.

Bungay is a medieval market town and is well worth a visit, if only to sample its antiquity, which has survived through its castle and two fine churches despite its "Great Fire" in 1688. The Buttercross was built a year later in 1689. The castle has recently been sold to the Town Trustees by the Duke of Norfolk.

This part of the Bigod Way now climbs to the Bath Hills which take their name from the 19th century bathing place. The Hills face south making a natural sun trap where spring flowers bloom earlier than anywhere else in England and nightingales sing here.

H. Rider Haggard, the Victorian author, lived in Ditchingham Lodge where he wrote wonderful adventure stories and delighted his generation.

Pass through the gate, cross the drive of Ditchingham Lodge, then uphill through pine trees to a stile. Cross and follow a well marked path which bends sharply left after a while and emerges finally into a tarmac lane. Go ahead in the lane downhill to a gate near Coldbath House.

On the way you pass the cottage of Lilias Rider Haggard, daughter of H. Rider Haggard. Lilias was a noted author in her own right and a close observer and commentator of Norfolk country life among ordinary folk.

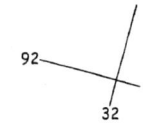

Pass through the gate and follow a grassy track which passes a cottage and enters its drive, which you follow to a road.

Continue past gravel pits, but just past three cottages on your right, turn left into hedged path which ends in a lane. Turn right to a bypass. The Earsham bypass follows the railway track of the one-time Waveney line.

Turn right at the bypass to a junction and cross the road to a metal slip stile by the one-time railway station and into a cul-de-sac. Continue into the centre of Earsham by the Queen's Head PH. Cross the road and go past the village hall, between houses, towards the church and into a road.

Turn left and, just before a humped bridge, turn right into a narrow fenced path which leads along the edge of a straight drainage cut from the Bungay Marsh to the River Waveney.

Cross two bridges into a meadow. Go leftwards over the meadow to a bridge. Cross and go rightwards towards a farm and to a stile, then into a lane which leads to a road.

Cross the road and up the right edge of a field to the top of a rise. A rest here will be rewarded by excellent views of the valley.

Follow the headland, keeping the hedge to your right, through right and left turns, passing The Dell and turning left along the top edge of the field to a gap and through into the next field.

Turn right to the perimeter of a disused airfield. Turn left to go southerly and past a farm, then turn left across a narrow strip of field to pass through a gap in a belt of woodland, into a tarmac track near a corner.

Turn right for a long $1/4$ mile to a junction in a dip near Shadowbarn Farm. Cross into a field and follow its left edge for about 350 yards to a small pond.

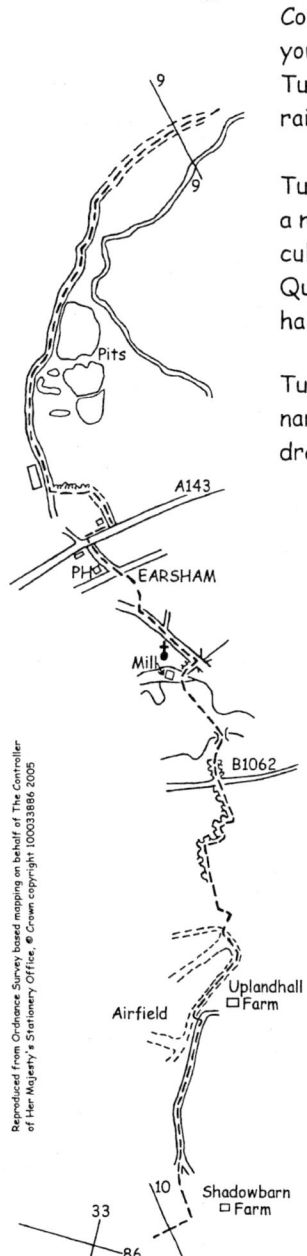

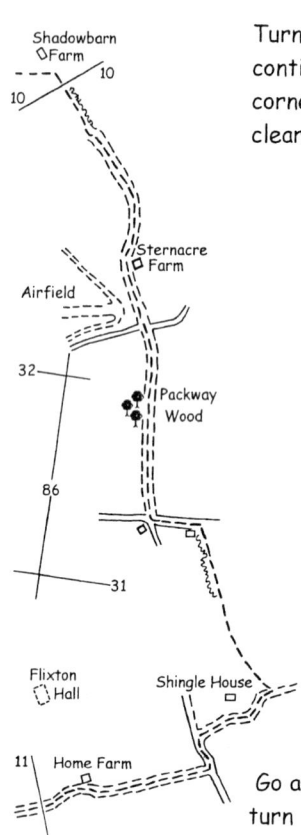

Turn right and straight across the field to meet a hedge and continue with it on your left. Shortly before you reach a field corner go into a green track on your left, follow it as becomes clearer and bends past Sternacre Farm to a road.

Cross into a lane past Packway Wood to a road by a thatched cottage. Turn left and, just past a pair of cottages, turn right and follow field edges to a gap.

Pass through and follow a short left edge, then straight ahead to follow the left edge of a ditch, then a short way over the field into a bridle track. Turn right, past the aptly named Shingle House to a road.

Turn left to a farm, then turn right into a bridle track through Flixton Park.

The Hall in Flixton is now a fire-damaged ruin. It was built in the reign of Henry VIII. An aircraft museum is located in the village behind the Buck Inn.

The road continues for $1/4$ mile, then bending right around the perimeter of Hall Farm then left.

Go ahead to a crossing of tracks and turn left with the flooded sandpits on your right.

After a $1/4$ mile, when in sight of a gate across the track, turn right between a high embankment and fenced trees and in a few yards join the B1062.

Turn left on the road, pass a road on the left and then bear left into Homersfield.

Turn left along the lane leading past St. Mary's Church to a woodland path and out to a road. Turn right along the road and soon left for Mendham.

At the next junction turn right and, where the road is closest to the river by the edge of a wood, turn right into a track.

This fine route leads to a stile, cross, turn down a bank, then leftwards along the edge of a field over another stile, then a short path leads into a lane uphill passing Downs Farm where you turn right into a track.

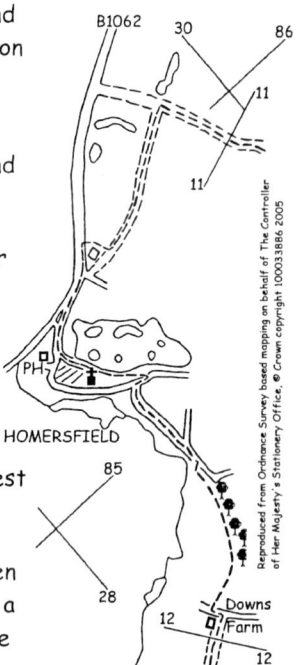

Go past the farm buildings and along a green lane to a gate. Pass through and follow a field's right edge at the foot of the hill, but, just before another gate, cross a stile on your right. Go ahead to cross a bridge, bear right to follow a field's right edge to a road. Turn right into Mendham.

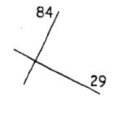

Alfred Munnings, nationally known artist famous for painting horses, was born here. Southwards lie Mendham marshes and the site of a 12th century Cluniac priory.

From the crossroads at the village sign, turn right for Harleston, then over the Waveney.

After about 150 yards turn right through the second gate, across a field diagonally, past an electricity pole to a stile near a gate in a corner and out to a road.

Turn right and soon left and up the right edge of a field. When the ditch bends sharply right continue ahead over the field, then with a ditch on your left to a copse. Join a well defined track leading to a stile and over to a bypass. Cross the bypass and over a stile to follow a track through a farm to join a minor road on the edge of Harleston.

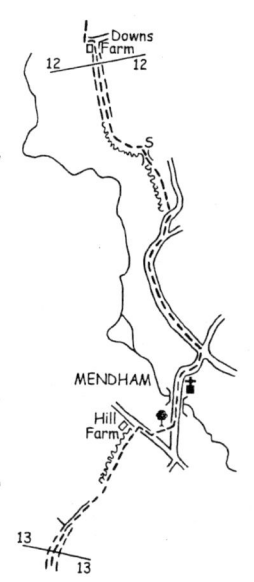

Continue your direction to a bend, *those wishing to visit the town go straight ahead, otherwise* after passing Lime Close (left) and Mendham Close (right), turn sharply left into a lane by a grey gabled house. Go straight along the lane, over Woodlands Road. Continue along a footpath on the right edge of a field to join a minor road, turn left for about 50 yards and turn right in a footpath to a stile on the bypass.

Cross the road into a path which descends with a fence on its left to Halesworth Road. Turn right and soon left for Brockdish for about 500 yards, then left, down a slope and through a kissing gate.

Cross a meadow diagonally to a bridge over a dyke, cross, turn left and follow the dyke to a bridge in the far corner. Cross into a gravel track, past a house and a wall on your right. Continue with a fence on the right and turn right into a metalled road. Just past the second house on your left, take the right hand track between field and wood. Continue your direction for about 700 yards to a gate.

Reproduced from Ordnance Survey based mapping on behalf of The Controller of Her Majesty's Stationery Office, © Crown copyright 100033886 2005

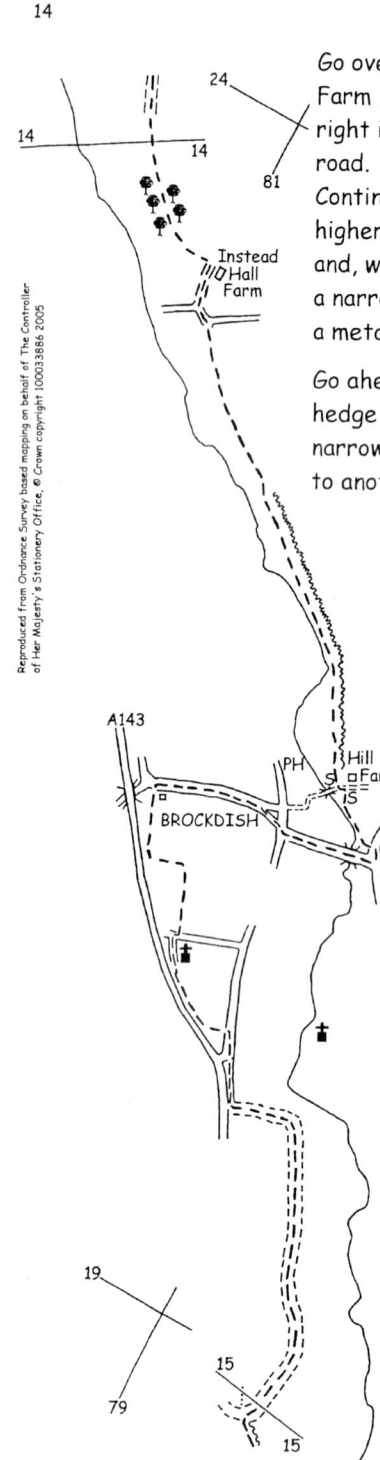

Go over the stile and bear left in a track to Instead Hall Farm *(this track may be exceedingly muddy after rain)*. Turn right into the farm road for about 250 yards to a minor road. Turn left for about 30 yards, then right over a stile. Continue south westerly with a fence on your right and higher ground on your left. After crossing two more stiles and, when a shallow ditch on your right ends, go ahead into a narrow field, continue between trees and ditch and over a metal gate.

Go ahead in a green lane, through a long meadow with a hedge on your left, then through a wooded section and narrow field to a stile. Go diagonally right across a field to another stile and into a track.

(O.S. maps may show a right turn through a game packing station, then looping around to the east of Brockdish.) Turn left for about 30 yards then right over a stile. Go ahead, first with a hedge on your left, then on right, down through a gate, over a footbridge and along a wooded path to a minor road. Turn right and soon right again, cross the Waveney and continue to the old main road in Brockdish.

Turn right and then left over the footbridge adjacent to the ford, follow the road out of the village. Just before the road goes under the bypass and opposite Hall Road, turn left into a footpath alongside a cottage. Go uphill following a hedge on your right along a field, at the end of a copse on a rise, turn left to a second copse, bear rightwards along a field edge to a road.

Turn right, then left along a lane past Brockdish Church, continue along edge of sports field with hedge on your right. Go through a wire gate and turn left on a footpath alongside the bypass, continue to a hedge and bear left to a road.

Turn right, but as the road bends to meet the bypass go ahead along a stopped up road. At its junction with the new road turn left into a track. After another 350 yards the track turns right and continues in a south westerly direction with the Waveney flood meadows on your left.

After a mile the track turns towards the A143, but in 40 yards leave it by the 3rd gateway on the left. Continue along the field edge in south westerly direction, with hedge on left, cross a plank bridge, turn immediately left, then follow a boundary round to your right to a field corner. Bear right again after glimpsing the Waveney on your left, and follow boundary to river.

Hoxne is the site of a Paleolithic settlement, and gives its name to the Hoxnian inter-glacial period. It was here that in AD 870 King Edmund was slain by the Danes and the largest ever find of treasure trove was found recently by a man with a metal detector looking for lost farm tools. Today the village makes a pleasant diversion, with the opportunity for a lunch time drink. The Mid Suffolk Way starts from here.

Follow the bank to meet a crossing hedge, pass through and continue ahead with trees and occasional glimpses of the river on left. At the next corner go through hedge, cross a footbridge and turn right into broad green lane, at its end pass to left of pumping station.

Turn left onto redundant section of road and where this meets A143 turn right into Kiln Lane for upper Billingford. After about 350 yards turn left into a track going westwards, with a thorn hedge left, a wood and then a pasture right. Continue past the hall and into a concrete drive to a metalled road.

Billingford Mill is on your left.

Turn left a few yards and turn right into a field. Go uphill along the right edge, past oaks to a metalled road on a bend. Turn right, with the remains of a ruined church on your left.

After $1/4$ mile, just beyond semi-detached cottages on your right turn left over a stile into a field, first along a left edge, then straight across to a gate. Continue in line over the next field to corner, turn right over a stile then shortly left. Continue on left edge for 100 yards, then, by a gap in hedge, bear right diagonally across field to emerge on the old A140, with Lodge Farm on your right.

Cross the road and go ahead on an unclassified road over new A140. Continue on the road for $1/2$ mile, then turn left opposite the Moat House.

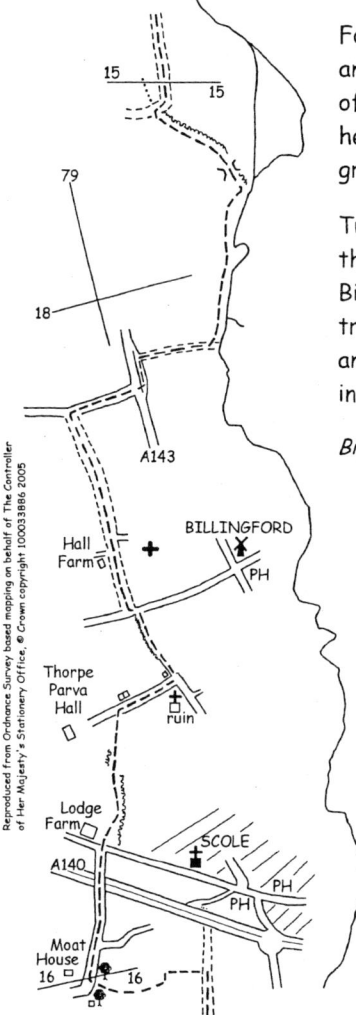

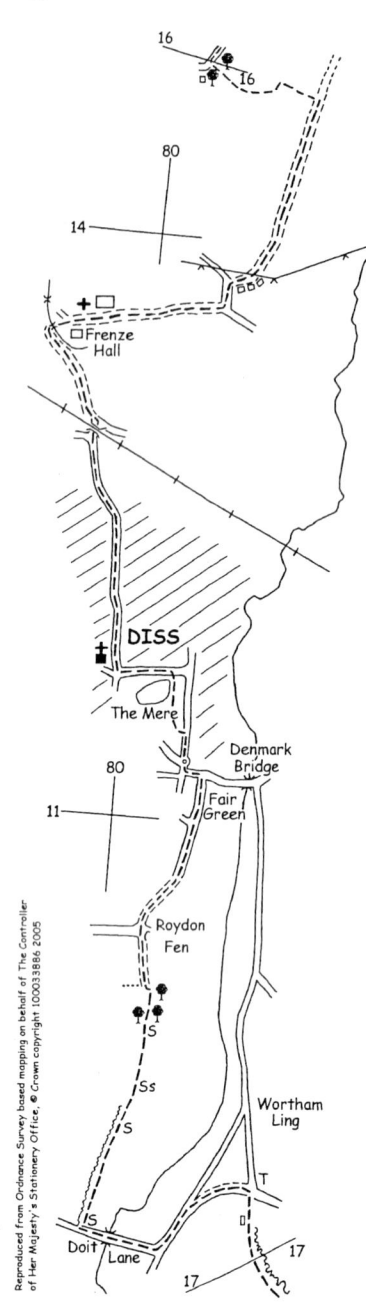

Go through a belt of trees into field, turn right around edge. On 3rd side, instead of passing into next field ahead, bear right over dry ditch and follow a left edge down to Miller's Lane. Turn right, continue for $3/4$ mile, under power cables and past houses to a road on a corner.

Bear left and, when the road bends sharply left, turn right into a driveway for Frenze Hall. Pass a church, then bear left over a bridge, turn left to join a track. Turn right on a metalled road, go under a railway bridge and follow the road into Diss by the church.

Diss has a rich selection of historic buildings, many dating from the 16th and 17th centuries and some with even older origins. It has an attractive townscape, greatly enhanced by the Mere, a $5\,1/2$ acre natural lake probably formed 10,000 years ago by the collapse of a bed of chalk. It is enjoyed by a fine selection of waterfowl.

Turn left along Mere Street and take a path on your right, passing to the left of the Mere, to a car park on the A1066.

Turn right, then, just beyond the roundabout, left into Lower Denmark Street. Take the first right, along Fair Green and follow into Tottington Lane, bear left along Roydon Fen (cul-de-sac).
The route shown on some O.S. maps, along the road between Denmark Bridge and Wortham Ling, was a solution to a temporary problem, now resolved.

When you reach the gates at the end of Roydon Fen Street bear left around the bottom of a garden. The path leads through a copse, over a stile and along a field edge to two more stiles. Cross continue your direction along a track, over another stile, then a field edge to Doit Lane.

Turn left to follow Doit lane for about $1/3$ mile, turn left at T junction, then either follow the road, forking right after about 300 yards, or cross the Ling in a similar direction keeping the road to your left. When you reach a junction with a phone box turn right onto a footpath by a post box in a wall.

Follow the narrow path then bear to the left of a thatched cottage go over a stile and continue, curving gently left, with a hedge on your left. When the field narrows, go over a stile by a gate in the corner, continue ahead to go over two more stiles to the left of gates, bear to the right diagonally across the field to another stile and footbridge.

Continue in line to a kissing-gate in a corner near the church, keep to the left through churchyard to the side gate and road and turn right. Just as the road bears very slightly to the left after about 250 yards take a footpath to the right.

The path goes slightly leftwards across to the outer corner of a hedged field boundary, where it meets a track coming from the right. Join the track to go ahead then quickly left.

At cross tracks go ahead, bearing slightly right, and continue to the road. Turn left for 150 yards then turn right on a track. Follow the track as it bends to the left of a new plantation then through a gap at the bottom of a field, continue ahead with ditch on your right, down to the next field boundary at the bottom of the dip, turn right with the ditch on your left, follow the track crossing the ditch, continue to the road by Dashes Farm.

Turn left, following the road round sharp right and left bends. Turn right on a narrow path just beyond a second bungalow, with a beech hedge. Cross the Waveney, turn left on the riverside path into Redgrave Fen.

The path through Redgrave Fen is by permission of the Suffolk Wildlife Trust. The Fen is the home of the rare Great Raft Spider, but you are more likely to see the Polish Tarpan horses, their grazing helps to control the vegetation. Be prepared for an occasional diversion or temporary closure.

Continue along the riverbank for just over half a mile, then cross a bridge on your left. Follow the path, firstly along the Fen boundary, then bend right. Keep to the path, ignore an access track on your left, and continue through a wood, then left to a road. If you wish to visit Redgrave cross into Mill Lane, otherwise turn right to crossroads.

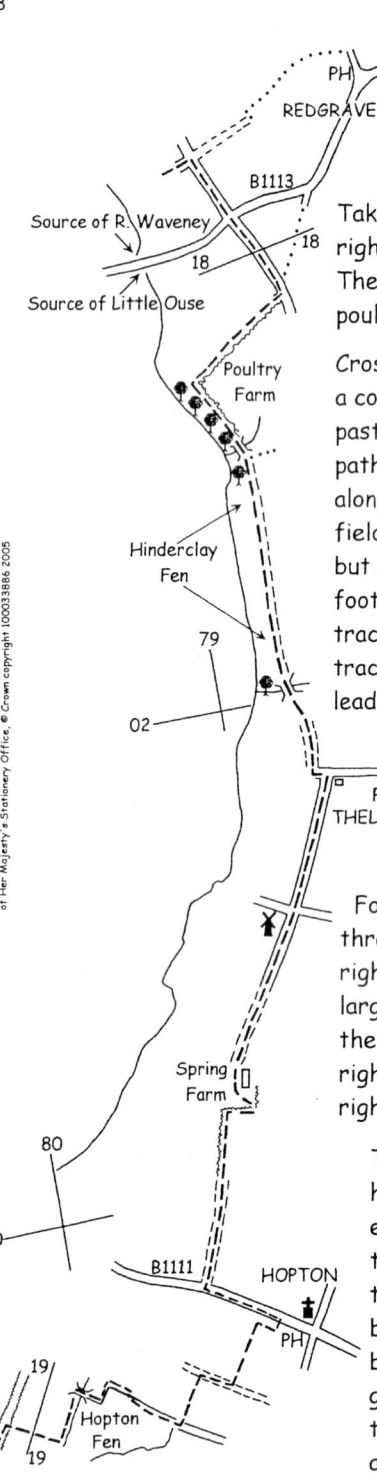

The sources of the River Waveney and Little Ouse are on either side of the road a $1/4$ mile to your right. A most unusual watershed in woodland carr, but the Waveney flows east and the Little Ouse flows west. The County boundary follows both infant rivers.

Take the road for Hinderclay for $1/4$ mile and turn right into a track between a field and new house. The path eventually turns sharply left behind the poultry farm into a green track to a bridge.

Cross and bear right in a path through the middle of a copse, leftwards to continue close to a field and past heathland to a crossing track. Go over into a path past blackthorn and closely past gorse, then along the edge of Hinderclay Fen to the end of a field on your left. Go a short distance with the path, but soon fork right through woodland carr. Cross a footbridge and go straight over a field into a green track through woodland carr and reed swamp. The track eventually bends sharply left into a road leading to Thelnetham.

Refreshments at the White Horse PH straight ahead, otherwise turn right after 100 yards, continue to, and over, a cross-roads by a tower mill.

Follow an unfenced road to Spring Farm and through the farmyard. Leave the track as it swings right, pass close to the house then keep left of a large barn to a gap in a corner, up into the field, then turn right through the hedge and follow the right edge. At field corner turn left, keeping to right edge, into a track and to B1111 in Hopton.

Turn left for $1/4$ mile and turn right in a narrow hedged path opposite Orchard House. At the end of gardens, turn right for 100 yards then turn left for 300 yards across fields into a farm track. Turn right for 200 yards, then left beside a hedge to a green lane at the field bottom. Turn right and soon through a kissing gate into Hopton Fen. A path follows the edge of the Fen, then climbs a bank into a field, turn along left edges to a footbridge.

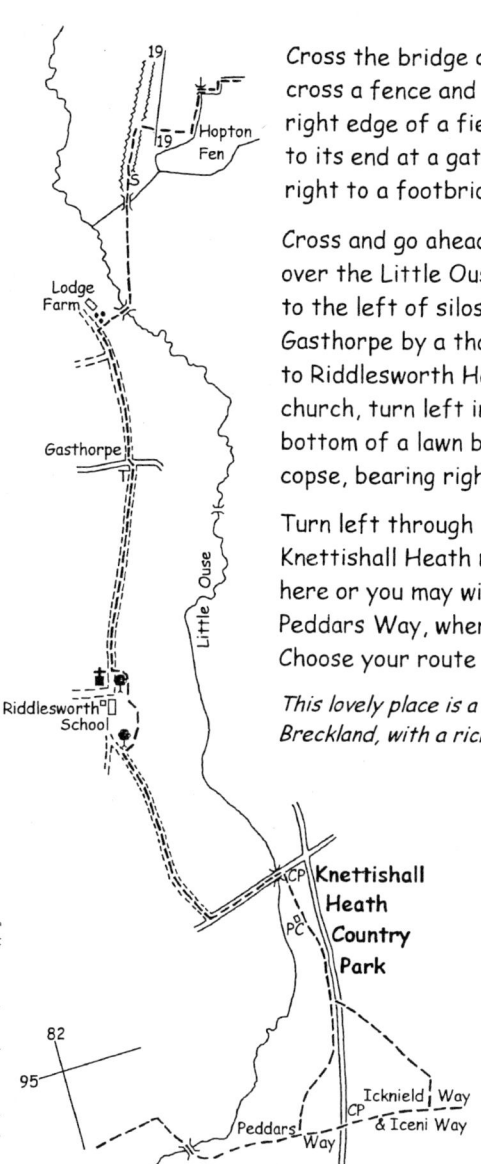

Cross the bridge and turn left along a stream to oaks, cross a fence and bend rightwards through gorse. Follow a right edge of a field, through a gate and turn left in a lane to its end at a gate. Cross a stile on your left and turn right to a footbridge.

Cross and go ahead for $1/2$ mile, then across a footbridge over the Little Ouse. Go ahead to cross a low bridge, then to the left of silos into a road. Turn left for $1/2$ mile into Gasthorpe by a thatched cottage. Cross into a rough lane to Riddlesworth Hall (now a school), but, shortly before the church, turn left in a path through a copse, then along the bottom of a lawn below the Hall. Continue between field and copse, bearing right until you meet a sandy track.

Turn left through parkland and out to a road. Turn left to Knettishall Heath main car park — you may finish your walk here or you may wish to connect with the beginning of the Peddars Way, where there is another small car park. Choose your route across the heath.

This lovely place is a well preserved portion of historical Breckland, with a rich variety of trees, including some noble pines.

If you wish to keep walking take the first section of the Iceni Way (way-marked as *"Angles Way Link"*) adding 16 miles and continuing the route to Thetford, with a good selection of accommodation and good transport links.

Knettishall is a junction of Long Distance Paths:- Three-quarters of mile to the west of the main car park is the start of the PEDDARS WAY AND NORFOLK COAST PATH. You could now set off for Cromer and then, by WEAVERS WAY to Great Yarmouth to complete a Round Norfolk Walk.

On your left another challenge, the ICKNIELD WAY ending at Ivinghoe Beacon where it joins the Ridgeway to Avebury and eventually to Lyme Regis.

The ICENI WAY commences here, at the end of the Angles Way, it joins the route of the Icknield Way, but then swings north to rejoin the Little Ouse at Thetford. It follows the Little and Great Ouses all the way to King's Lynn, then goes on to Hunstanton where it meets the Norfolk Coast Path - so allowing the option of an even longer Round Norfolk Walk.

Details of availability of guide books for all the above and other routes are shown on page 28.

Mileage Chart and Transport Planner

```
. Knettishall Heath (Thetford Station 6 miles  Harling Road Station 7 miles) Σ ◊  (π Home Farm Riddlesworth 1 mile)
 4.1  . Hopton Vine P.H. (Garboldisham 2 miles)
 7.6   3.5  . B1113 crossroad north of Redgrave
10.9   7.4        . Diss Ø (Station .75 mile)
15.0  10.8   7.4   3.4  . Scale Lodge Farm (Ø Garage .75 mile)
18.4  14.3  10.8   7.4   3.4  . Brockdish Greyhound Ø
24.5  20.4  16.9  13.2   9.5   6.1  . Harleston (ØΔ Parish Church)
28.2  24.1  20.6  16.9  13.2   9.8   3.7  . Homersfield (ØΔ A143 Dove Restaurant)
32.4  28.3  24.8  20.6  17.4  14.0   7.9   4.2  . Earsham Queen's Head Δ #
39.0  34.9  31.4  24.0  24.0  20.6  14.5  10.8   6.6  . Ditchingham (ØΔ Maltings)
42.1  38.0  34.5  27.1  27.1  23.7  17.6  13.9   9.7   3.1  . Shipmeadow Old Church Δ
46.5  42.4  38.9  31.5  31.5  28.1  22.0  18.3  14.1   7.5   4.4  . Beccles Old Market ØΔ # (Station .5 mile)
49.4  45.3  41.8  34.4  34.4  31.0  24.9  21.2  17.0  10.4   7.3   2.9  . Oulton Broad South Station (# Dutchman's Corner)
58.6  54.5  51.0  43.6  43.6  40.2  34.1  30.4  26.2  19.6  16.5  12.1   9.2  . Oulton Broad North Station
59.3  55.2  51.7  44.3  44.3  40.9  34.8  31.1  26.9  20.3  17.2  12.8   9.9   0.7  . Somerleyton Station
64.3  60.2  56.7  49.3  49.3  45.9  39.8  36.1  31.9  25.3  22.2  17.8  14.9   5.7   5.0  . Fritton Country Park (ØΔ Decoy Tavern)
68.9  64.8  61.3  53.9  53.9  50.5  44.4  40.7  36.5  29.9  26.8  22.4  19.5  10.3   9.6   4.6  . Burgh Castle Church
73.2  69.1  65.6  58.2  58.2  54.8  48.7  45.0  40.8  34.2  31.1  26.7  23.8  14.6  13.9   8.9   4.3  . Great Yarmouth Station
78.0  73.9  70.4  63.0  63.0  59.6  53.5  49.8  45.6  39.0  35.9  31.5  28.6  19.4  18.7  13.7   9.1   4.8    (ØΔ Market Gates)
```

Mileages are measured from small scale maps and are approximate

NOTES

"Station" = railway service. For details phone:- One Railway 0845 600 7245. www.onerailway.com There is no direct train service between North and South stations at Oulton Broad. (Oulton Broad North station is about 200 yards off route)

Σ = Peddars Wayfarer Bus. Thetford - Bus Stn. 09.55 + 14.25, Railway Stn. 10.00 + 14.30 to Knettishall Heath. Knettishall Heath 13.09 + 17.39 to Thetford. Daily from late March to end October. (Times valid in 2005 check for subsequent years). www.nationaltrail.co.uk 01328 850530

◊ = Brecks Bus will provide transport between Thetford & Knettishall, Monday to Friday 0900- 16.00 (service may be extended to longer hours and include weekends). Book by phone 01842 816170, before noon, day before journey.

π = Bus service 191 (college days only). Early morning Diss - Thetford. Early evening Thetford - Diss, both via Home Farm, Riddlesworth (GR 959820) (1ml. 1.5km by minor road to Knettishall Heath).

Ø = Bus service 580 runs Mon-Sat between Great Yarmouth and Diss, includes pick up points at Fritton, Beccles (with connections to Lowestoft), Ditchingham, Bungay, Earsham, A143 (near Homersfield), Harleston,Brockdish, Billingford, Scole, Diss Station. Some buses do not cover the whole route.

∆ = Bus service 581 runs Mon-Sat (once a day each way) between Great Yarmouth and Harleston, includes pick up points at Fritton, Beccles, Barsham, Shipmeadow, Bungay, Earsham, A143 (near Homersfield).

= Bus service 173 runs Mon-Sat (once a day each way) Earsham, Bungay, Ditchingham, Beccles, Lowestoft.

Details of these and other bus services in the area from: TraveLine - phone 0870 606 2608, www.traveline.org.uk Services and timetables are liable to change at short notice, so it is important to check before setting out.

21

Accommodation and Amenities List

Places that provide accommodation or refreshments on or near the route have been included for your convenience when planning your walk. The list is neither complete nor selective and its accuracy cannot be guaranteed. Some listings for accommodation are up to two miles from the route (or more if they are willing to pick you up from the route and take you back the next morning. - see below). Please notify us of any mistakes or places which you think should be included or deleted. Thank you for your help.

Prices are not specified (except tent pitches) as they are subject to change, but we do show an approximate guide to both costs (based on prices in 2005) and likely standard of facilities.

The following abbreviations are used:-

AW	On or very close to route	GH	Guest house	Sh	Shop
BB	Bed & Breakfast	GR	Grid reference	Shw	Showers
B/d	Onward baggage delivery	H	Hotel	S/n	No smoking
B/m	Bar meals	I	Inn	S/r	Smoking restrictions
C	Campsite	L	Launderette	T.	Telephone
D	Double room	PH	Public house	T/p	Tent pitches
D/f	Drying facilities	P/l	Packed lunches by arrangement	Tw	Twin room
Dgs	Dogs by arrangement	PO	Post Office	V	Vegetarian menu available
ECD	Early closing day	P/u	Pick up service	YH	Youth hostel
EM	Evening meal	R	Restaurant		Approximate price guide*:-
F	Family room	S	Single room	£+	Lower & mid range
F.	Fax	S/c	Self catering	£++	Higher range

Arrangements for a pick up service or baggage delivery should always be made in advance. Charges will vary. Establishments providing a pick up service may prefer you to stay more than one night.
Establishments open throughout the year (possibly excluding Christmas/New Year) unless otherwise stated.
* Price guide based on two people sharing a room, singles may be substantially more expensive

GREAT YARMOUTH Norfolk (STD 01493)
YH   YHA, 2 Sandown Road, NR30 1EY T.0870 770 5840 F./5841 40 beds
Please contact the Tourist Information Office at Town Hall, Hall Plain, Great Yarmouth.
(T 846345/842195) for an accommodation list for Great Yarmouth.

BURGH CASTLE Great Yarmouth, Norfolk (STD 01493)
C +   Burgh Castle Marina, Butt Lane, NR31 9PZ. T.780331 F.780163 www.burghcastlemarina.co.uk
PH + R   GR 475041. 10 T/p from £14 , Shw, L. Apr-Oct.   Fisherman's Free House PH, R + B/m. Apr-Nov.
+ Info.   Information + Exhibition Centre (in Reception) for Roman ruins + marshland heritage.   AW
C + R   Breydon Water Holiday Park, , NR31 9BQ. T.780357/780481.
    Restaurant (open to non-residents out of peak season).
PO+Sh   Butt Lane, NR31 9AJ. T.780269. General Store. Cash withdrawals with some bank cards.
    Open 9.00-13.00 + 14.00-17.00 Mon-Sat. Extended hours in Summer + Sunday mornings.

BELTON Great Yarmouth, Norfolk (STD 01493)
PH   The Tavern, Station Road. T.780286. Bar snacks (except Friday).
C   Wild Duck Holiday Park, Howard's Common, NR31 9NE. T.780268 F.782308. GR 475025
R   130 T/p from £6. Shw, L, D/f, Dgs,
Sh   Sh 7 days, takeaways 12-14-00 + 17.00-24.00. R, PH, snack bar, 7evenings.
C   Rose Farm Touring Park, Stepshort, NR31 9JS T.780896. GR 488034
    www.rosefarmtouringpark.co.uk   40 T/p £10-£12 (special rates seniors) Shw, Dgs.

FRITTON Great Yarmouth, Norfolk (STD 01493)

PH Decoy Tavern, Beccles Road, NR31 9AB. T.488277. B/m. 7 days 11.00-14.00 + 18.30-22.00. Dgs.

ST. OLAVES Norfolk (STD 01493)

PH + R Bell Inn, Beccles Road, NR31 9HE T.488249 F.488424 www.bellinn-stolaves.co.uk V, Dgs, R + B/m. Lunch & evening 7 days.

PO+Sh General Store. 7 days a week.

R Priory Farm Restaurant, Beccles Road, NR31 9HE T.488432 F.488479 R + snacks. 7 days 12.00-14.00 + 18.15-20.30 (Saturday to 21.30)

SOMERLEYTON Suffolk (STD 01502) - (Note: BR train service available from here back to Yarmouth or into Lowestoft for overnight accommodation.)

PH Dukes Head, Slugs Lane. T.730281. Meals and bar snacks.

PO+Sh The Street. General Store.

BB Waveney Grange Farm, Station Road, NR32 5QL. T.730258. GR 484968 www.lothingland.page.co.uk carolyn@greerwalker.freeserve.co.uk 1D, 2Tw S/r, P/l, Dgs, D/f, P/u, B/d. £+ AW

BLUNDESTON Suffolk (STD 01502)

BB Oak Farm, Market Lane, NR32 5AP. T.731622. GR 523980 1D, 1Tw. £+

PH Plough Inn, Market Lane, T.730261

OULTON Lowestoft, Suffolk (STD 01502)

H + R Parkhill Hotel, Parkhill, NR32 5DQ T.730322 F.731695 GR 530959 www.parkhillhotel.co.uk 11D, 7Tw, 2S, 5F EM, V, P/l, S/r, Dgs, D/f, P/u. £++ Restaurant 12.30-13.45 & 18.30-21.00

BB Laurel Farm, Hall Lane, NR32 5DL. T.568724. GR 519948 www.laurelfarm.com 3D, 2T. (poss. S or F), P/l, S/n, D/f. Self catering kitchen if req. £+

OULTON BROAD Lowestoft, Suffolk (STD 01502)

H George Borrow Hotel, Bridge Road, NR23 3LL. T.569245. 6D, 4Tw, 4S, 3F. R. EM.

H + R Ivy House Country Hotel, Ivy Lane, NR33 8HY. T.501353 F.501539 www.ivyhousecountryhotel.co.uk GR 512922 14D, 4Tw, 1S, 1F, EM, V, P/l, S/r (some rooms), Dgs, D/f, B/d. £++ (reduced prices Sundays) Self catering also available. Crooked Barn Restaurant 12.00-13.45 & 19.00-21.30. AW

LOWESTOFT Suffolk (STD 01502)

Please contact the Tourist Information Office, Waveney District Council, Town Hall, High Street, Lowestoft, (T.523000) for an accommodation list for Lowestoft.

GELDESTON Norfolk (STD 01508 Kirby Cane)

PH Locks Inn, Locks Lane. T.518414. Meals and bar snacks Friday - Sunday only at present

BECCLES Suffolk (STD 01502) Tourist Information Centre T.713196

H+R The King's Head Hotel, New Market NR34 9HA. T.712147. www.elizabethhotels.co.uk 3Tw, 1S, 1F, Dgs. £++ Meals and bar snacks.

H+R + PH Waveney House Hotel, Puddingmoor, NR34 9PL, T.711477 F.470370 www.waveneyhousehotel.co.uk 9D, 3Tw, EM, V, P/l, S/n, D/f, £++ R Mon-Sat.19.00-21.00. B/m daily 12.00-14.00 + 18.30-21.00 AW

PH+BB The Bear & Bells, Old Market, NR34 9AP. T.715545. 1D. Meals, beer garden. CAMRA award.

BB + C Sue & Graham Bergin, Pinetrees, Park Drive, Worlingham, NR34 7DQ. T.470796 www.pinetrees.net GR 435900 3D, V, P/l, S/n, D/f, £+ Campers welcome in 5½ acre field (no Shw).

BB Catherine House, 2, Ringfield Rd, NR34 9PQ. T./F. 716428 2D, 1F, V, D/f, P/l, S/r, £+ AW

BB Saltgate House, 5 Saltgate, NR34 9AN. T.710889 www.saltgatehouse.co.uk 3Tw, 1F. £+/£++

GH + R Colville Arms Motel, Woodland Ave. Lowestoft Rd, NR34 7EF T.712571 www.colville-arms-motel.co.uk 2Tw, 1S, 1F. £+/£++ Bar & restaurant

C Beulah Hall Caravan Park, Dairy Lane, NR34 7QJ T.476609 F.476453 GR 479893 (nr. Barnby) carol.stuckey@fsmail.net GR 479892 Dgs, Shw. 30 T/p £8 -£10

C Waveney Lodge, Elms Road, Aldeby, T.677445

BROOME Bungay Norfolk (STD 01508)

BB Broome Lodge, Loddon Road, NR35 2HX T.518177 F.518717 www.broomelodge.co.uk 3Tw. £+

DITCHINGHAM Bungay Norfolk (STD 01986)

PH   The Duke of York, 8 Norwich Road. T.895558. Meals and bar snacks.

BUNGAY Suffolk (STD 01986)   Tourist Information, Council Offices, Earsham Street, T.892176

H+R   King's Head Hotel, Market Place, NR35 1AW T.893583 www.kingsheadhotel.biz 7D, 2Tw, 1F, £+
      R daily 12.00-14.00 (Sun 12.00-15.00) & Tues-Sat 18.30-20.00. Snacks daily 10.00-17.00

BB   Bigod Holidays, 22 Quaves Lane, NR35 1DF T.892907 bigodholidays@care4free.net
      1D, 1Tw, 1S, P/l, S/n, D/f, P/u, B/d, £+

I   Castles Inn, 35 Earsham Street, NR35 1AF T./F.892283 3D, 1Tw, Dgs. £+/£++ Restaurant.

I   Angel Inn, 1 Lower Olland Street, NR35 1BY   £+

BB   Ann Woolston, T.896016 www.annwoolston.com (on B10562 w. edge of Bungay). 1D, 1S, D/f, EM by
      arrangement, Dgs. (outside kennel), £+

BB   Mr. M.E. Tate, Fairfield House, 36 Fairfield Road, NR35 1RY. T.893897   malcolm.tate@talk21.com
      D/f, 1D, 1Tw. £+

C   Outney Meadow Caravan Park, NR35 1HG T.892338 F.896627 GR 333903
      Shw, Dgs. 45 T/p £9-£13

Misc. PO, shops, banks, PH, restaurants etc. takeaway food, launderette

EARSHAM postal address Bungay Suffolk (STD 01986)

BB   Earsham Park Farm, Old Railway Road, NR35 2AQ. T.892180 www.earsham-parkfarm.co.uk
      GR 304883 2D, 1Tw. P/l, S/n, Dgs, D/f, P/u. Lift to pub for EM. £+

PH   Queens Head, Station Road. T.892623. Bar snacks.

FLIXTON Suffolk (STD 01986)

BB   Ray & Jane Sharp B & B, Ye Olde Post Office, The Street, NR35 1NZ. T.893187   1D, 1Tw, 1S. P/l,
      S/n, D/f, £+ (nr. Aviation Museum),

PH   Flixton Buck

HOMERSFIELD Harleston, Norfolk (STD 01986)

BB   J. Hunt, Heath Farmhouse, IP20 0EX. T.788417. 2D, 1Tw/F, EM, V, P/l, S/r, D/f, P/u, B/d, £+   AW

PH R Black Swan, Church Lane, IP20 0ET T.788204   F.788179 R + B/m lunch + evening 7 days
+ C   Campsite, 5 T/p, dgs, no Shw, £6 per night   AW

ALBURGH Norfolk (STD 01986)

BB+R Dove Restaurant, Holbrook Hill, Alburgh, IP20 0EP. T.788315. www.thedovenorfolk.co.uk
      1D, 1Tw. P/l, Dgs. £+ Note: situated close to Homersfield Bridge) AW

WORTWELL Harleston, Norfolk (STD 01986) (W. of Homersfield)

C   Little Lakeland Caravan Park, IP20 0EL T./F.788646 www.littlelakeland.co.uk GR 280850
      15T/p £9.30 - £13.60, Shw, Sh,

PH   The Bell, 52 High Road, IP20 0HH   Meals 12.00 - 14.00 (not Monday) & 19.00 -21.00

MENDHAM Harleston, Norfolk (STD 01986)

BB   Weston House Farm, IP20 0PB T.782206 GR 292828. 2Tw, S/n, Dgs, £+

HARLESTON Norfolk (STD 01379)

H   Swan Hotel, 19 The Thoroughfare, IP20 9DQ   T.852221   harlestonswan@btopenworld
      10D, 4Tw, Dgs. £++

H+R   J D Young Hotel, 2-4 Market Place, IP20 9AD. T.852822 F.855370   9D, 1Tw, 1S. EM, V, P/l, S/r,
      Dgs, £++   R + B/m - lunch + evening 7 days

PH   Cherry Tree, 74 London Road, IP20 9BZ   T.852345

PH   Duke William, 28 Redenhall Road, IP20 9ER T.853183

BB   Mrs. Frewin B & B, Millhouse Potteries, 1 Station Road, IP20 9ES. T.852556. 1D, 1Tw, 1S.
      V, P/l, D/f, £+

WEYBREAD postal address Norfolk (STD 01379)

PH   The Crown Inn, Weybread, Nr. Diss, Norfolk. IP51 5TL. T.586710. 1D, 1Tw, 1F, £+/£++
 +BB Meals & bar snacks Tuesday to Saturday, Sunday lunch only. (EM Sunday by arrangement with BB)

BROCKDISH Diss, Norfolk (STD 01379)

PH R The Old Kings Head, The Street, IP21 4JY T./F. 668125 theoldkingshead@hotmail.com 1D, 1Tw,
+BB   EM, V, P/l, Dgs, £+   R & B/m lunch & evening 7 days. Take-away fish & chips.
BB   Grove Thorpe, Grove Road, IP21 4JR. T.668305 www.grovethorpe.co.uk   £+/£++
S/c   Jackie & John Spooner, The Old Coach House, The Street, IP21 4JY T.668146
       4 cottages - short breaks available.

HOXNE Suffolk (STD 01379)

PH + R The Swan, Low Street, IP21 5AS T.668275 www.hoxneswan.co.uk R + B/m, V, garden 7 days
        12.00-14.30 + 19.00-21.30 (Sunday 12.00-16.00 + 19.00-21.00) pre-order for large parties. Dgs.
PO S   Hoxne PO Stores, Low Street, IP21 5AR. T./F. 668254   Snacks, hot/cold drinks, Open Mon-Fri
        7.30-17.30 (Fri to 18.30) excl. lunch 13.00-14.00 + ECD Wednesday. Sat 8.00-12.30, Sun 8.30-11.00

BILLINGFORD Norfolk (STD 01379)

I   The Horseshoes, Lower Road, IP21 4HL T.740414 F.740146 1D, EM, V, P/l, D/f, £++
        R + B/m Monday -Saturday 11.30 - 21.00, Sunday 12.00 - 19.45

SCOLE Norfolk (STD 01379)

C   Willows Camping & Caravan Park, Diss Road, Scole, Diss, IP21 4DH. T./F.740271. Shw, 16 T/p
        from £6 per night. May-September.
H   Scole Inn, Ipswich Road, Scole, IP21 4DR. T.740481. F.740462, 18D, 3Tw, 2F, EM, Dgs, £++
        R + B/m lunch + evening 7 days.
PH + R Crossways Inn, Bridge Road, Scole, IP21 4DP. T./F.740638. R + B/m. Snacks, meals, coffee all day
        from 10.00, 7 days.

DISS Norfolk (STD 01379) ECD Tuesday
Information available from Tourist Information Centre, T.650523

BB   Gill Robinson, Greenways, 25 Frenze Rd, IP22 4PB T.642147 2D, 1Tw, S/n, D/f, P/u, B/d, £+ AW
PH   Saracens Head, 75, Mount Street, Diss, IP22 4QQ. T.652853.
+BB   3F, 1D, 1Tw, some en-suite. Meals and bar snacks. Real ale. Large car park.   AW
PH   Waterfront Inn, 43 Mere Street, Diss, IP22. T.51076. Meals + bar snacks (lunch only).   AW
H + R   The Park Hotel, 29 Denmark Street, IP22 4LE. T.6422244 F.644218 www.parkhoteldiss@aol.com
        10D, 6Tw, 4S, 2F, EM, S/r, Dgs, D/f, £++   R + B/m   AW
BB   Koliba Guesthouse, 8 Louie's Lane, IP22 4LR T.650046 www.koliba.co.uk GR 113802 , 1D, 1Tw, 1S,
        EM, P/l, S/r, D/f, P/u, B/d, £+   AW
Misc.   PO, banks, shops, launderette, cafes, take-aways (Fish & chips, Indian, Chinese).

FAIR GREEN, Diss, Norfolk (STD 01379)

take   Fair Green Fish Bar, Lower Denmark Street. T.642412 . Mon-Sat. 12.00-14.30 + 17.00-23.00
away   Sun. 12.00-14.30 + 17.00-21.00   AW
Cafe   Angel Café, 1 Fair Green, IP22 4BQ. T.741067. www.angelcafe.co.uk Tues-Fri 9.30-17.00,
        Sat. 10.00-17.00, Sun. 10.00-16.00. (Closed Monday) AW
R+BB   Fayreview Restaurant, 65 Lower Denmark Street, IP22 3LG.   T.644684   AW
PH   Cock Inn, 63 Lower Denmark Street, Fair Green, IP22 3LG. T.643633. No food.   AW

PALGRAVE Diss, postal address Norfolk (STD 01379)

BB   Mrs. Windsor, Brambley House, Lion Road, Palgrave, IP22 1AL. T.641666. 1F, 1D, 1Tw, 1S. P/l

ROYDON Norfolk (STD 01379)

PH + R White Hart, High Road, IP22 5RU T.643597. R + B/m. Mon-Sat. 12.00-15.00 + 18.00-21.00
        Sun 12.00-21.00

BRESSINGHAM Diss, Norfolk (STD 01379)

BB   Mrs. Soar, Poplar Farm, IP22 2AP. T.687261. 1D, 1Tw, 2S.   No dogs.
BB   David & Pat Bateson, Lodge Farm, Algar Road, IP22 2BQ. T.687629. 1F, 1D, 1Tw. Simple meals by
        prior arrangement.
PH   The Chequers, Thetford Road. T.687405. Meals and bar snacks (not Monday).

WORTHAM postal address Diss, Norfolk (STD 01379)
- BB Rookery Farm, Old Bury Road, IP22 1RB. T.783236 3Tw. £+
- C   Honeypot Caravan & Camping Park, IP22 1PW. T./F.783312 www.honeypotcamping.co.uk
      GR 086772 T/p (incl. hot water) from £12 (2 people) Shw. Sh & tearoom 100yds PH 200yds

REDGRAVE postal address Norfolk (STD 01379)
- PH Cross Keys Inn, The Street, IP22 1RW T.898510 F.897297 www.crosskeysredgrave.co.uk
      GR 045780 R + B/m, P/l, Lunch - not Monday. Evening meals - not Sunday/Monday.
      Cash back available with purchase, and mobile phone e-top up.

SOUTH LOPHAM Norfolk (STD 01379)
- BB Paddie & Mark Miller, Oxfootstone Granary, Low Common, IP22 2JS. T.687490 GR 052810
      2Tw, (both en-suite). No EM - lift to pub if required £+
- BB Malting Farm, Blo' Norton Road, IP22 2HT. T.687201   GR 035808   3D. £+

RICKINGHALL postal address Norfolk (STD 01379)
- I R The Bell Hotel, The Street, IP22 1BN. T.898445 www.thebellrickinghall.com 3D, 4Tw, 1S, EM, V,
       P/l, D/f, £+   R + B/m lunch + evening.
- BB   Grangers B & B, Garden House Lane, IP22 1EA. T.897210 www.grangersbandb.co.uk GR 045754
       1D, 1Tw/F. P/l, S/n, D/f, P/u, B/d, £+
- Misc Fish & chips, Chinese takeaway, PHs.

THELNETHAM postal address Norfolk (STD 01379)
- PH The White Horse, Hopton Road. T.898298. Meals and bar snacks.

HOPTON postal address Norfolk (STD 01953).
- PH R Vine Inn, High Street, IP22 2QX T.681466 Meals
- GH   The Old Rectory, IP22 2QX T.688135 www.wolseylodges.com 1D, 1Tw. EM, residents alcohol license
        Dgs, £++ closed Easter (& Xmas/New Year)
- PO+S Chandlers Village Supermarket. Open 8.30 to 5.00 Monday to Saturday (except ECD Wednesday)

GARBOLDISHAM Diss, Norfolk (STD 01953)
- BB   Ingleneuk Lodge, Hopton Road, IP22 2RQ. T.681541 www.ingleneuk-lodge.co.uk GR 003802
       2D, 2Tw, 1S, B/m (by arrangement) residents alcohol license V, P/l, S/r, Dgs, D/f, P/u, B/d, £++ ,
- Taxi Rod Middleton T.681541. rod@rodmid.freewire.co.uk Any length of journey. Advance booking

KNETTISHALL HEATH (STD 01953)
- C   Camping for backpackers only. Country Park Warden - T.688265. No shop or cafe.
      Light refreshments sometimes available in good weather from mobile vans on car park.

CONEY WESTON Bury St. Edmunds, Suffolk
- BB   Barbara Clarke, Lundy Cottage, Thetford Road, IP31 1DN T.221906 peterclarke1001@hotmail.com
        1D, 1Tw. P/l, S/n D/f, P/u, B/d
- PH C The Swan, Thetford Road, IP31 1DN T.221295. jack.stimpson@btinternet.com Snacks. Tent space

WEST HARLING East Harling, Norwich Norfolk (STD 01953)
- C Dower House Touring Park, NR16 2SE. T.717314 F.717843 www.dowerhouse.co.uk GR 969853
     60 T/p from £9. Shw, L, Sh, Dgs. PH/R, take-away meals, swim pool, (all campers only). Mid Mar-Sept.

EAST HARLING Norwich Norfolk (STD 01953) 6 miles via forest paths & Peddars Way.
- PH R Nags Head, Market Street, NR16 2AD T.718140   Restaurant - lunch + evenings, 7 days
- BB   2D, 2Tw, EM, V, S/r. £+
- PH   Swan Inn T.717951 meals
- BB   The Old Dairy, White Hart Street, NR16 2NE T.717687 www.olddairyharling.co.uk
        1D, 2Tw, 1F. P/l S/n, £+
- Misc PO, shops, Chinese take-away, fish & chips.

SHADWELL Nr. Thetford, Norfolk (STD 01842) by River Thet, 2 miles along Peddars Way
- C Thorpe Woodlands Camp Site, Shadwell, IP24 2RX. T.751042 (Forest Enterprises) Small charge
     Toilet/washroom, no Shw, limited shop. Large parties. Open Easter to late October.

NEW BUCKENHAM Norwich Norfolk (STD 01953) (Note. Use of pick-up service essential)
BB   Pump Court, Church Street, NR16 2BA. T.861039 F.861153 www.pump-court.co.uk. 1D, 1Tw, 1F. P/l, S/n, D/f, P/u, B/d. £+
PH   The George, Chapel Street. T.860043
PH   The King's Head, Market Place. T.860487

BARNHAM Suffolk STD 01842) (Iceni Way)
BB   Mrs. Margaret Heading, East Farm, Barnham, IP24 2PB. T.890231 F.890457
1D. 1Tw, P/l, S/n D/f, P/u £+

THETFORD (STD 01842) 6 miles by road or 16 miles via Iceni Way to Knettishall Heath
H R   Bell Hotel, King Street, IP24 2AZ T.754455 F.755552. www.bellhotel-thetford.com
16D, 13Tw, 11S, 1F + 5 feature rooms. EM, V, P/l, S/r, £++
I R   Anchor Hotel, Bridge Street, IP24 3AE T.763925 F.766873 www.eurotrailhotels.com 9D, 3Tw, 4S, 2F, EM, V, P/l, S/r, Dgs, D/f, £++ R + B/m. £++
H   Wereham House Hotel, 24 White Hart Street. IP24 1AD T.761956 F.765207
www.werehamhouse.co.uk   4D, 2Tw, 1S, 1F, EM, V, P/l, S/n (except bar) £++
BB   M. Findlay, The Pink Cottage, 43 Maadalen Street, IP24 2BP T.764564
maggie.findlay1@btopenworld.com   2Tw, 1S, P/l, D/f, £+
Misc.   PO, shops, banks, PHs, restaurants etc. take-away food, launderette

Connecting Long Distance Paths

Most guide books will be available in Tourist Information Offices and local bookshops, but guide books and/or information may also be obtained from:-

BOUDICA'S WAY - Public Rights of Way Officer, South Norfolk District Council, Swan Lane, Long Stratton, Norfolk, NR15 2XE T.01508 533684 www.south-norfolk.gov.uk

FEN RIVERS WAY - Ramblers Association - Cambridge Group, 52 Maids Causeway, Cambridge, CB5 8DD. £4.50 incl. p. & p.

GIPPING VALLEY PATH - Suffolk County Council, Planning Department, St. Edmunds House, Rope Walk, Ipswich. T.01473 583174

HEREWARD WAY - Cambridge County Council Environment & Transport, Shire Hall, Castle Hill, Cambridge, CB3 0AP. T.01223 717445 www.cambridgeshire.gov.uk Leaflet 30p + A5 SAE

ICKNIELD WAY - Icknield Way Association, 19, Boundary Road, Bishop's Stortford, Herts. CM23 5LE. www.icknieldway.co.uk e-mail - info@icknieldway.co.uk
Walkers' Guide £4.50 plus postage. Accommodation Guide £1 plus s.a.e.

ICENI WAY - Ramblers' Association, Caldcleugh, Cake Street, Old Buckenham, Attleborough, NR17 1RU T.01953 861094 Guide £3 incl. p. & p.

LITTLE OUSE PATH [Thetford to Brandon] - Brecks Countryside Project, Kings House, King Street, Thetford. T.01842 765400 www.brecks.org Guide - Walking in the Brecks £2

MARRIOTT'S WAY - Norfolk County Council, Planning & Transportation, County Hall, Martineau Lane, Norwich, NR1 2SG T.01603 222769 www.countrysideaccess.norfolk.gov.uk

MID SUFFOLK PATH - Project Officer, Mid Suffolk District Council, Needham Market, IP6 8DL T.01449 727294

NAR VALLEY WAY - Norfolk County Council, Planning & Transportation, County Hall, Martineau Lane, Norwich, NR1 2SG T.01603 222769 www.countrysideaccess.norfolk.gov.uk

PASTON WAY - Norfolk County Council, Planning & Transportation, County Hall, Martineau Lane, Norwich, NR1 2SG T.01603 222769] www.countrysideaccess.norfolk.gov.uk

PEDDARS WAY & NORFOLK COAST PATH - Ramblers' Association, Caldcleugh, Cake Street, Old Buckenham, Attleborough, NR17 1RU T.01953 861094 Guide £3 incl. p. & p.

ST. EDMUND WAY - John Andrews, 6, Priory Close, Ingham, Bury St. Edmunds, Suffolk, IP31 1NN. Guide £4.25 incl. p. & p.

STOUR VALLEY PATH - Dedham Vale & Stour Valley Project, Suffolk County Council, Environment & Transport Dept., County Hall, Ipswich, IP4 1LZ T.01473 583176

SUFFOLK COASTAL PATH - Project Officer, Suffolk Coast & Heaths Project, Dock Lane, Melton, Woodbridge, IP12 1PE T.01394 384948 www.suffolkcoastandheaths.org

WAVENEY WAY — Ramblers' Association, 1, Church Close, Redenhall, Norfolk, IP20 9QS T.01379 852572 Guide £2.50 incl. p. & p.

WEAVERS' WAY - Included in Peddars Way & North Norfolk Coast Path Guide (see above).

WHERRYMAN'S WAY - Norfolk County Council, Planning & Transportation, County Hall, Martineau Lane, Norwich, NR1 2SG T.01603 222769 www.countrysideaccess.norfolk.gov.uk